Drool-Worthy Burrito and Chimichanga Recipes

Loaded Flavor-Busting Wraps to Enjoy for Days

By: Tyler Sweet

License Page

Table of Contents

Introduction

Sometimes, all you need is a comforting meal that requires nearly no effort. You may have some leftovers in the fridge and maybe thinking up a fun way to use them. Burritos and chimichangas are excellent inlets for them.

This cookbook shares some fantastic burritos and chimichangas that we know you'll be loving for days. So, to make life simple and fun for you, we chose the simplest makes that are ultimately delicious, nutritious, splurge-worthy, and satisfying.

Each recipe shares a burrito and chimichanga option, so you can easily switch things. What's more, you'll only need to gather your ingredients and let's get to creating some amazing pieces.

Are you ready to make lunch a fun thing? Yup! We heard you. Let's get into it then.

1. Cheesy Bacon Breakfast Burritos / Chimichangas

Make breakfast a full pack of goodness. Thankfully, tortilla wraps can hold the ingredients up nicely and make your morning perfect.

Prep Time: 20 mins

Cook Time: 18 mins (burritos) + 6 mins (chimichangas)

Serves: 4

Ingredients:

Burritos:

- 8 slices bacon
- 1 (16 oz) package frozen hash browns
- 8 large eggs
- ⅓ cup milk
- 2 tbsp butter
- Salt and black pepper to taste
- 4 large flour tortillas, burrito size
- ½ cup shredded cheddar cheese
- 1 ripe avocado, pitted, peeled, and sliced
- Hot sauce, for serving

Chimichangas:

- Vegetable oil for frying
- Hot sauce for serving

Instructions:

Burritos:

Heat a skillet over medium heat. Add bacon and cook for 8 to 10 minutes or until golden brown. Transfer bacon to a paper towel-lined plate and chop into small bits.

Add hash browns to skillet and cook for 5 minutes or until golden brown. Transfer to a plate and set aside.

Crack eggs into a bowl, add milk, and season with salt and black pepper. Beat smoothly. Melt butter in the same skillet, pour in eggs and scramble until set.

Lay tortillas on a clean, flat surface and spread hash browns, eggs, bacon, cheddar cheese, and avocado. Fold in the sides and roll up the ends to secure.

Slice in halves and serve with hot sauce.

Make it chimichanga:

Keep burritos whole.

Heat ½-inch of oil in a deep skillet and add two burritos. Fry for 3 minutes per side or until golden brown and crispy.

Transfer chimichangas to a paper towel-lined plate to drain grease. Fry the other two burritos the same way.

Serve with hot sauce.

2. Sweet Potato and Beans Burritos / Chimichangas

It is an excellently vegan meal featuring natural sweetness from sweet potatoes and a filling punch of black beans.

Prep Time: 20 mins

Cook Time: 10 mins (burritos) + 6 mins (chimichangas)

Serves: 4

Ingredients:

Burritos:

- 2 tsp olive oil
- 1 large onion, diced
- 2 garlic cloves, minced
- 1 tsp cumin powder
- 1 tsp dried oregano
- 1 tsp chili powder
- 1 tsp paprika
- 1 (15 oz) can black beans, drained and rinsed
- Salt and black pepper to taste
- 4 large tortillas, burrito size
- 2 medium sweet potato, peeled cooked, and mashed
- 2 tomatoes, diced
- 1 avocado, pitted, peeled, and sliced
- 1 tbsp chopped fresh cilantro
- 1 lime, cut into wedges for serving
- ½ cup sour cream

Chimichangas:

- Vegetable oil for frying
- Sour cream for serving

Instructions:

Burritos:

Heat olive oil in a skillet over medium heat. Add onion, cook for 3 minutes and add garlic; cook for 30 seconds or until fragrant. Season with cumin powder, oregano, chili powder, paprika, and cook for 1 minute. Stir in black beans, season with salt, black pepper, and simmer for 5 minutes or until warmed.

Lay tortillas on a clean, flat surface and spread sweet potatoes on top. Add beans mixture, tomatoes, avocado, and cilantro. Fold in the sides and roll up the ends to secure.

Slice in halves and serve with lime wedges and sour cream.

Make it chimichanga:

Keep burritos whole.

Heat ½-inch of oil in a deep skillet and add two burritos. Fry for 3 minutes per side or until golden brown and crispy.

Transfer chimichangas to a paper towel-lined plate to drain grease. Fry the other two burritos the same way.

Garnish with cilantro, top with sour cream, and serve.

3. Shredded Chicken Burritos / Chimichangas

It is a classic Mexican chicken made using leftover chicken and shredding them to perfection. The deal is in the seasoning mix.

Prep Time: 20 mins

Cook Time: 17 mins (burritos) + 6 mins (chimichangas)

Serves: 4

Ingredients:

Burritos:

- 2 tbsp olive oil
- ½ cup diced yellow onion
- 2 garlic cloves, minced
- 1 (15 oz) can diced tomatoes with green chilies
- 1 tablespoon chili powder
- 1 tbsp cumin powder
- ¼ tsp cayenne pepper (optional)
- 1 tbsp smoked paprika
- Salt and black pepper to taste
- 3 cups cooked shredded chicken
- 4 large tortillas, burrito size
- ½ cup chicken broth
- 1 cup shredded Mexican cheese blend
- 2 tbsp chopped fresh cilantro

Chimichangas:

- Vegetable oil for frying
- Sour cream for serving
- Chopped fresh cilantro for garnish

Instructions:

Burritos:

Heat olive oil in a skillet over medium heat. Add onion and sauté for 3 minutes. Stir in garlic and cook for 30 seconds or until fragrant. Stir in tomatoes, chili powder, cumin powder, paprika, cayenne pepper, salt, and black pepper. Cook for 10 minutes and stir in chicken and broth. Simmer for 3 minutes to warm the chicken. Adjust taste with salt and black pepper.

Lay tortillas on a clean, flat surface and spread chicken on top. Add Mexican cheese blend and cilantro. Fold in the sides and roll up the ends to secure.

Slice in halves and serve.

Make it chimichanga:

Keep burritos whole.

Heat ½-inch of oil in a deep skillet and add two burritos. Fry for 3 minutes per side or until golden brown and crispy.

Transfer chimichangas to a paper towel-lined plate to drain grease. Fry the other two burritos the same way.

Drizzle with sour cream and garnish with cilantro.

Serve warm.

4. Beef and Rice Burritos / Chimichangas

What fun way to fill up in the afternoon? It is a resemblance to beef and rice casserole but this time it is conveniently packed for easy carrying along.

Prep Time: 20 mins

Cook Time: 17 mins (burritos) + 6 mins (chimichangas)

Serves: 4

Ingredients:

- ½ tbsp olive oil
- ½ onion, diced
- 2 garlic cloves, minced
- 1 lb. ground lean beef
- 1 tsp onion powder
- 1 tsp dried oregano
- 2 tsp paprika
- 2 tsp cumin powder
- ¼ tsp cayenne pepper or to taste (optional)
- Salt and black pepper to taste
- 2 tbsp tomato paste
- 3 tbsp water.
- 4 large tortillas, burrito size
- 2 cups warm cooked rice
- 2 cups shredded cabbage
- 1 cup black beans, drained and rinsed
- 1 cup corn kernels, drained
- 3 tomatoes, finely chopped
- 1 cup shredded cheddar cheese
- 1 tbsp chopped fresh cilantro

Chimichangas:

- Vegetable oil for frying
- Sour cream for serving
- Chopped fresh cilantro for garnish

Instructions:

Burritos:

Heat olive oil in a skillet over medium heat. Add onion and sauté for 3 minutes. Stir in garlic and cook for 30 seconds or until fragrant. Stir in beef, onion powder, oregano, paprika, cumin powder, cayenne pepper, salt, and black pepper. Cook for 10 minutes and stir in tomato paste and water. Simmer for 3 minutes and adjust taste with salt and black pepper.

Lay tortillas on a clean, flat surface and spread cabbage and rice on top. Add beef, black beans, corn, tomatoes, cheddar cheese, and cilantro. Fold in the sides and roll up the ends to secure.

Slice in halves and serve.

Make it chimichanga:

Keep burritos whole.

Heat ½-inch of oil in a deep skillet and add two burritos. Fry for 3 minutes per side or until golden brown and crispy.

Transfer chimichangas to a paper towel-lined plate to drain grease. Fry the other two burritos the same way.

Drizzle with sour cream and garnish with cilantro.

Serve warm.

5. Beans and Cheese Burritos / Chimichangas

Have you had beans and cheese before? If not, then these tasty wraps show you just how to. It is a super delicious treat.

Prep Time: 20 mins

Cook Time: 10 mins (burritos) + 6 mins (chimichangas)

Serves: 4

Ingredients:

Burritos:

- 1 (16 oz) can refried beans
- ¼ medium onion, diced
- ½ cup chunky salsa
- ½ tsp smoked paprika
- ½ tsp garlic powder
- Salt and black pepper to taste
- 4 large tortillas, burrito size
- ½ cup shredded cheddar cheese
- ½ cup shredded Monterey Jack cheese

Chimichangas:

- Vegetable oil for frying
- Tomato sauce for serving

Instructions:

Burritos:

In a pot, combine refried beans, salsa, paprika, garlic powder, salt, and black pepper. Stir and cook over medium heat for 10 minutes or until beans warm through. Turn heat off.

Lay tortillas on a clean, flat surface, spread beans on top, and add cheeses. Fold in the sides and roll up the ends to secure.

Slice in halves and serve.

Make it chimichanga:

Keep burritos whole.

Heat ½-inch of oil in a deep skillet and add two burritos. Fry for 3 minutes per side or until golden brown and crispy.

Transfer chimichangas to a paper towel-lined plate to drain grease. Fry the other two burritos the same way.

Serve warm with tomato sauce.

6. Brown Rice and Beans Burritos / Chimichangas

Pack up lunch in the most convenient and ethical way. Rice and beans stuffed into tortilla wraps are healthy, vegan, and help you prep lunch easily.

Prep Time: 20 mins

Cook Time: 14 mins (burritos) + 6 mins (chimichangas)

Serves: 4

Ingredients:

Burritos:

- 1 tbsp olive oil
- 1 small onion, diced
- 2 garlic cloves, minced
- 1 (7 oz) can tomatoes with green chilies
- 1 cup black beans, drained and rinsed
- Salt and black pepper to taste
- 4 large tortillas, burrito size
- ½ cup corn kernels, drained
- Lime wedges for serving

Chimichangas:

- Vegetable oil for frying

Instructions:

Burritos:

Heat olive oil in a skillet over medium heat. Add onion and sauté for 3 minutes. Stir in garlic and cook for 30 seconds or until fragrant. Stir in tomatoes, black beans, salt, and black pepper. Cook for 10 minutes or until beans warm through.

Lay tortillas on a clean, flat surface and spread rice on top. Add beans mixture and corn kernels. Fold in the sides and roll up the ends to secure.

Slice in halves and serve with lime wedges.

Make it chimichanga:

Keep burritos whole.

Heat ½-inch of oil in a deep skillet and add two burritos. Fry for 3 minutes per side or until golden brown and crispy.

Transfer chimichangas to a paper towel-lined plate to drain grease. Fry the other two burritos the same way.

Serve warm.

7. Steak Burritos / Chimichangas

Gather some leftover steak from the previous dinner and work it into this delicious treat. It is a simple composition but fantastic.

Prep Time: 10 mins

Cook Time: 6 mins (chimichangas)

Serves: 4

Ingredients:

Burritos:

- 4 large tortillas, burrito size
- 12 ½ cups leftover steak strips, shredded and warmed
- 1 small onion, chopped
- 1 cup shredded queso cheese
- 1 cup cooked brown rice, warmed
- 1 cup guacamole
- 1 (15 oz) can refried beans, warmed
- 1 cup salsa
- ¼ cup chopped fresh cilantro

Chimichangas:

- Vegetable oil for frying
- Sour cream for topping
- Pico de gallo for topping

Instructions:

Burritos:

Lay tortillas on a clean, flat surface and spread steak strips, onion, queso cheese, brown rice, guacamole, refried beans, salsa, and cilantro on top. Fold in the sides and roll up the ends to secure.

Slice in halves and serve.

Make it chimichanga:

Keep burritos whole.

Heat ½-inch of oil in a deep skillet and add two burritos. Fry for 3 minutes per side or until golden brown and crispy.

Transfer chimichangas to a paper towel-lined plate to drain grease. Fry the other two burritos the same way.

Top with sour cream and pico de gallo.

Serve warm.

8. Beef, Bean, and Sausage Burritos / Chimichanga

If beef wasn't enough, then adding sausage and beans would give you that ultimate satisfaction that you crave. Even better, avocado adds some natural creaminess.

Prep Time: 20 mins

Cook Time: 24 mins (burritos) + 6 mins (chimichangas)

Serves: 4

Ingredients:

Burritos:

- 1 tbsp olive oil
- 8 oz Italian sausage, sliced
- 1 cup chopped onion
- 4 oz ground beef
- Salt to taste
- 1 (10 oz) can chopped tomatoes with chiles, undrained
- 1 (15.5 oz) can pinto beans, drained and rinsed
- 1 tsp chili powder
- 4 large tortillas, burrito size
- 1 cup shredded cheddar cheese
- ½ cup chopped lettuce
- 2 tomatoes, chopped
- 1 avocado, pitted, peeled, and sliced
- Sour cream for topping

Chimichangas:

- Vegetable oil for frying
- Sour cream for topping
- Chopped fresh cilantro for garnish

Instructions:

Burritos:

Heat olive oil in a skillet over medium heat. Add sausage and fry for 2 to 3 minutes per side or until golden brown. Transfer sausages to a plate.

Add ground beef to skillet and cook for 5 minutes. Season with salt and cook for 3 minutes. Stir in tomatoes, pinto beans, and chili powder. Simmer for 10 minutes.

Lay tortillas on a clean, flat surface and spread beef mixture, sausage, cheddar cheese, lettuce, avocado, tomatoes, and sour cream. Fold in the sides and roll up the ends to secure.

Slice in halves and serve.

Make it chimichanga:

Keep burritos whole.

Heat ½-inch of oil in a deep skillet and add two burritos. Fry for 3 minutes per side or until golden brown and crispy.

Transfer chimichangas to a paper towel-lined plate to drain grease. Fry the other two burritos the same way.

Top with sour cream and garnish with cilantro.

Serve warm.

9. Butternut Squash and Black Beans Burritos / Chimichangas

If you haven't explored using butternut squash other than as a side dish, these wraps are an excellent way to enjoy them. And they turn out mouthwatering.

Prep Time: 20 mins

Cook Time: 10 mins (burritos) + 6 mins (chimichangas)

Serves: 4

Ingredients:

Burritos:

- 2 tsp olive oil
- 1 small onion, chopped
- 1 medium red bell pepper, deseeded and chopped
- 2 garlic cloves, minced
- 1 tsp cumin powder
- ¼ tsp cayenne pepper
- 1 (15 oz) black beans, drained and rinsed
- Salt and black pepper to taste
- 4 large tortillas, burrito size
- 1 cup cubed and roasted butternut squash
- 1 cup cooked brown rice, warmed
- 1 cup grated vegan cheese
- 1 tbsp chopped fresh cilantro
- ½ cup salsa
- 1 avocado, pitted, peeled, and sliced

Chimichangas:

- Vegetable oil for frying

Instructions:

Burritos:

Heat olive oil in a skillet over medium heat. Add onion, bell pepper, and sauté for 3 minutes. Stir in garlic and cook for 30 seconds or until fragrant. Stir in cumin powder, cayenne pepper, and cook for 1 minute or until fragrant. Stir in black beans, salt, and black pepper; cook for 5 minutes or until beans warm through.

Lay tortillas on a clean, flat surface and top with butternut squash, brown rice, beans mixture, vegan cheese, cilantro, salsa, and avocado. Fold in the sides and roll up the ends to secure.

Slice in halves and serve.

Make it chimichanga:

Keep burritos whole.

Heat ½-inch of oil in a deep skillet and add two burritos. Fry for 3 minutes per side or until golden brown and crispy.

Transfer chimichangas to a paper towel-lined plate to drain grease. Fry the other two burritos the same way.

Serve warm.

Serve warm.

10. Taco Breakfast Burritos / Chimichangas

Let's make a breakfast party with this set. Taco seasoning pumps up the mood.

Prep Time: 20 mins

Cook Time: 19 mins (burritos) + 6 mins (chimichangas)

Serves: 4

Ingredients:

Burritos:

- 1 lb. ground beef
- 1 medium onion, diced
- 4 garlic cloves, minced
- 1 tbsp taco seasoning
- 1 jalapeno pepper, diced
- 1 tbsp olive oil
- 8 large eggs
- ⅓ cup half and half
- Salt and black pepper to taste
- 4 tbsp unsalted butter
- 4 large tortillas, burrito size
- 1 cup refried beans
- 1 large tomato, diced
- 1 cup shredded cheddar cheese
- 1 cup sliced American cheese
- Hot sauce (for serving)

Chimichangas:

- Vegetable oil for frying

Instructions:

Burritos:

Add beef to a pot and cook over medium heat for 8 minutes or until mostly brown. Stir in onion, garlic, taco seasoning, and jalapeno pepper; cook for 3 minutes or until tender. Turn heat off.

Crack eggs into a bowl, add half and half, salt, and black pepper. Whisk until smooth. Melt butter in a skillet over medium heat. Pour in eggs and scramble for 3 to 5 minutes or until set.

Lay tortillas on a clean, flat surface and spread refried beans on top. Add beef, eggs, tomato, and cheeses. Fold in the sides and roll up the ends to secure.

Slice in halves and serve with hot sauce.

Make it chimichanga:

Keep burritos whole.

Heat ½-inch of oil in a deep skillet and add two burritos. Fry for 3 minutes per side or until golden brown and crispy.

Transfer chimichangas to a paper towel-lined plate to drain grease. Fry the other two burritos the same way.

Drizzle with sauce and garnish with cilantro.

Serve warm.

11. Pumpkin Pie Burritos / Chimichangas

Introduce dessert early into the afternoon with this pumpkin puree-filled wraps. It is sweet with a comforting effect.

Prep Time: 20 mins

Cook Time: 6 mins (chimichangas)

Serves: 4

Ingredients:

Burritos:

- 1 (15 oz) can pumpkin puree
- 8 oz cream cheese, room temperature
- ¼ cup granulated sugar
- ½ tsp ginger powder
- 1 ½ tsp cinnamon powder
- ¼ tsp cloves powder
- 1 (21 oz) can apple pie filling
- 4 large tortillas, burrito size

Chimichangas:

- Vegetable oil for frying
- ¾ cup granulated sugar
- 1 ½ tsp cinnamon powder

Instructions:

Burritos:

In a bowl, mix pumpkin puree, cream cheese, ¼ cup of sugar, ginger powder, cinnamon powder, cloves powder, and apple pie filling until well-combine.

Lay tortillas on a clean, flat surface and spread on pumpkin mixture. Fold in the sides and roll up the ends to secure.

Slice in halves and serve.

Make it chimichanga:

Keep burritos whole.

Heat ½-inch of oil in a deep skillet and add two burritos. Fry for 3 minutes per side or until golden brown and crispy.

Transfer chimichangas to a paper towel-lined plate to drain grease. Fry the other two burritos the same way.

In a bowl, mix sugar and cinnamon powder. Sprinkle cinnamon sugar on chimichangas.

Serve warm.

12. Spicy Veggie Burritos / Chimichangas

Veggie burritos or chimichangas shouldn't be boring when there's some spice. Kick things up and enjoy a thrilling lunch.

Prep Time: 20 mins

Cook Time: 5 mins (burritos) + 6 mins (chimichangas)

Serves: 4

Ingredients:

Burritos:

- 2 tbsp olive oil
- 1 cup chopped onion
- 1 cup cubed zucchini, cubed
- 1 cup chopped red bell pepper
- 1 cup cubed squash, cubed
- 1 tbsp minced garlic
- 1 jalapeno pepper, chopped
- ½ tbsp taco seasoning
- 1 tsp paprika
- ½ tbsp oregano
- 1 tsp cayenne pepper
- 1 tsp red chili flakes
- 1 tsp fresh lemon juice
- Salt and black pepper to taste
- 4 large tortillas, burrito size
- 2 cups shredded Mexican cheese blend
- 1 avocado, peeled, pitted, and sliced
- 2 tomatoes, chopped
- 1 scallion, chopped
- Sour cream for serving

Chimichangas:

- Vegetable oil for frying

- Sour cream for topping
- Chopped tomatoes for garnish
- Chopped fresh scallions for garnish

Instructions:

Burritos:

Heat olive oil in a skillet over medium heat. Add onion, zucchini, bell pepper, and squash; cook for 3 minutes. Stir in garlic, jalapeno pepper, taco seasoning, paprika, oregano, cayenne pepper, red chili flakes, lemon juice, salt, and black pepper. Cook for 2 minutes or until fragrant and jalapeno is tender.

Lay tortillas on a clean, flat surface and spread vegetable mixture on top. Add avocado, tomatoes, and scallion. Fold in the sides and roll up the ends to secure.

Slice in halves and serve with sour cream.

Make it chimichanga:

Keep burritos whole.

Heat ½-inch of oil in a deep skillet and add two burritos. Fry for 3 minutes per side or until golden brown and crispy.

Transfer chimichangas to a paper towel-lined plate to drain grease. Fry the other two burritos the same way.

Top with sour cream and garnish with avocado, tomato, and scallion.

Serve warm.

13. Rotisserie Chicken Burritos / Chimichangas

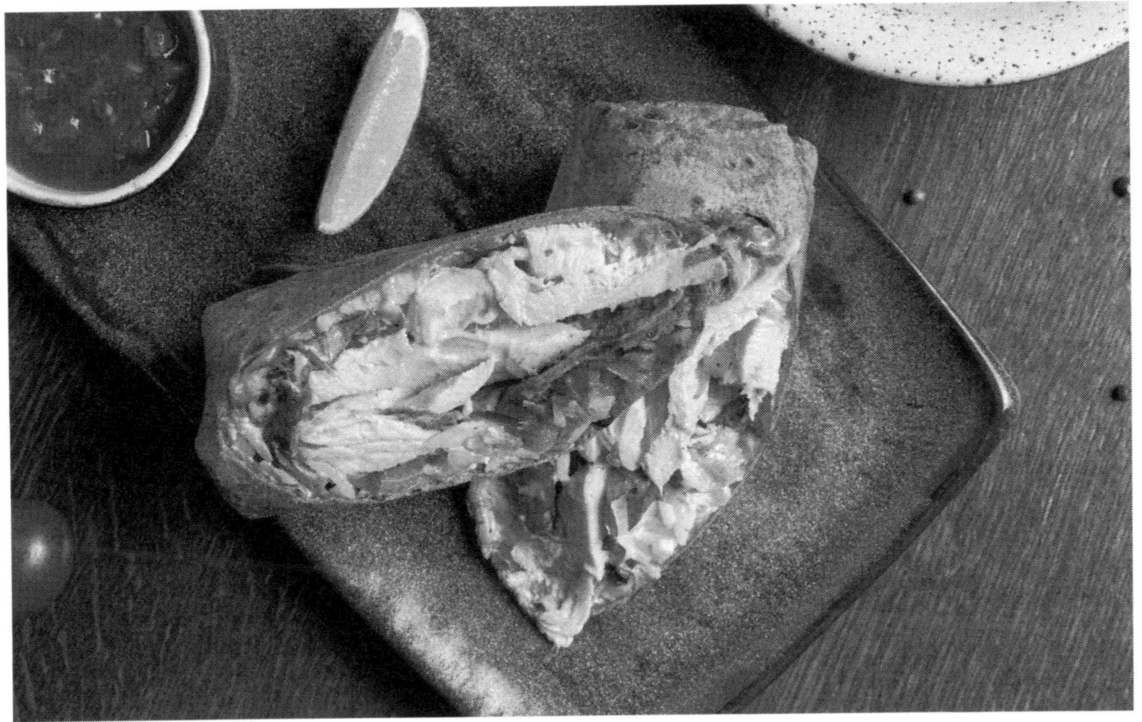

Grab some rotisserie chicken, add some rice, and beans and make it a worthy lunch.

Prep Time: 20 mins

Cook Time: 6 mins (chimichangas)

Serves: 4

Ingredients:

Burritos:

- 1 rotisserie chicken, white meat removed and shredded
- 1 tsp chili powder
- 2 tsp cumin powder
- Salt to taste
- 4 large tortillas, burrito size
- 1 cup cooked rice, warmed
- 1 (15 oz) can black beans, drained and rinsed
- ½ cup salsa
- 1 cup shredded cheddar cheese
- ½ cup sour cream
- 1 tomato, chopped
- 1 avocado, peeled, pitted, and diced

Chimichangas:

- Vegetable oil for frying
- Sour cream for topping
- Chopped basil or cilantro for garnish
- Chopped tomato for garnish
- Chopped avocado for garnish

Instructions:

Burritos:

In a bowl, mix chicken, chili powder, cumin powder, and salt.

Lay tortillas on a clean, flat surface and top with chicken, rice, black beans, cheddar cheese, and salsa. Fold in the sides and roll up the ends to secure.

Slice in halves and serve.

Make it chimichanga:

Keep burritos whole.

Heat ½-inch of oil in a deep skillet and add two burritos. Fry for 3 minutes per side or until golden brown and crispy.

Transfer chimichangas to a paper towel-lined plate to drain grease. Fry the other two burritos the same way.

Top with sour cream and garnish with basil or cilantro, tomato, and avocado.

Serve warm.

14. Creamy Chicken Burritos / Chimichangas

You would want more and more bites of this creamy goodness. It is everything a pamper is, you simply can't have enough.

Prep Time: 20 mins

Cook Time: 5 mins (burritos) + 6 mins (chimichangas)

Serves: 4

Ingredients:

Burritos:

- 3 cups shredded cooked chicken breasts
- 1 jalapeno pepper, chopped
- 2 (10.5 oz) cans cream of chicken soup, low-sodium
- 1 (8 oz) package cream cheese, room temperature
- 1 cup shredded Monterey Jack cheese
- 1 tsp paprika
- 1 tsp chili powder
- 1 tsp garlic powder
- ½ tsp cumin powder
- Salt and black pepper to taste
- 4 large tortillas, burrito size
- Sour cream for topping (quantity to taste)
- ½ cup shredded cheddar cheese for garnish
- 1 scallion, chopped for garnish

Chimichangas:

- Vegetable oil for frying
- Sour cream for topping (quantity to taste)
- ½ cup shredded cheddar cheese for garnish
- 1 scallion, chopped for garnish

Instructions:

Burritos:

In a pot, combine chicken, jalapeno, and cream of chicken soup. Cook over medium heat for 3 minutes or until boiling and chicken warms through. Reduce heat and stir in cream cheese, Monterey Jack cheese, paprika, chili powder, garlic powder, cumin powder, salt, and black pepper. Stir until cheeses melt and is creamy.

Lay tortillas on a clean, flat surface and spread creamy chicken on top. Fold in the sides and roll up the ends to secure.

Drizzle sour cream on top and garnish with cheddar cheese and scallion. Serve.

Make it chimichanga:

Keep burritos whole.

Heat ½-inch of oil in a deep skillet and add two burritos. Fry for 3 minutes per side or until golden brown and crispy.

Transfer chimichangas to a paper towel-lined plate to drain grease. Fry the other two burritos the same way.

Drizzle sour cream on top and garnish with cheddar cheese and scallion. Serve.

Serve warm.

15. Chicken and Peppers Burritos / Chimichangas

Bell peppers are known for their sweet aroma and right here, they shine through with some chicken.

Prep Time: 20 mins

Cook Time: 7 mins (burritos) + 6 mins (chimichangas)

Serves: 4

Ingredients:

Burritos:

- 2 tsp olive oil
- 1 red onion, peeled and sliced
- 1 each red and green bell pepper, deseeded and sliced
- 1 poblano pepper, deseeded and sliced
- ½ tsp garlic powder
- 1 tsp oregano
- 1 tsp smoked paprika
- ½ tsp cumin powder
- Salt to taste
- 2 cups shredded cooked chicken breasts
- 4 large tortillas, burrito size
- 1 can refried black beans
- Sour cream for topping to taste
- Guacamole for topping, to taste
- Salsa for topping, to taste
- 1 tbsp chopped fresh cilantro for topping

Chimichangas:

- Vegetable oil for frying
- Sour cream for topping to taste
- Guacamole for topping, to taste
- Salsa for topping, to taste
- Chopped fresh cilantro for garnish

Instructions:

Burritos:

Heat olive oil in a skillet over medium heat. Add onion, bell pepper, and poblano pepper. Sauté for 3 minutes or until tender. Stir in garlic powder, oregano, paprika, cumin powder, and salt. Cook for 1 minute or until fragrant. Mix in chicken and cook for 3 minutes or until warmed through.

Lay tortillas on a clean, flat surface and spread refried beans ton top. Spoon chicken mixture onto beans and add sour cream, guacamole, salsa, and cilantro. Fold in the sides and roll up the ends to secure.

Slice in halves and serve.

Make it chimichanga:

Keep burritos whole without sour cream, guacamole, salsa, and cilantro.

Heat ½-inch of oil in a deep skillet and add two burritos. Fry for 3 minutes per side or until golden brown and crispy.

Transfer chimichangas to a paper towel-lined plate to drain grease. Fry the other two burritos the same way.

Top with sour cream, guacamole, salsa, and cilantro.

Serve warm.

16. Green Chicken and Black Beans Burritos / Chimichangas

A little salsa verde tossed with some chicken and black beans make a world of difference in these wraps. Rather simple but with great tastes.

Prep Time: 20 mins

Cook Time: 6 mins (chimichangas)

Serves: 4

Ingredients:

Burritos:

- 2 ½ cups shredded rotisserie chicken
- 1 (4 oz) can green chilies, drained and rinsed
- ¼ cup salsa verde
- 1 (15 oz) can black beans, drained and rinsed
- Salt and black pepper to taste
- ¼ cup chopped fresh cilantro
- 4 large tortillas, burrito size
- 1 cup shredded Monterey Jack cheese
- Guacamole for serving
- Sour cream for serving
- Salsa for serving

Chimichangas:

- Vegetable oil for frying
- Guacamole for serving
- Sour cream for serving
- Salsa for serving

Instructions:

Burritos:

In a bowl, mix chicken, green chilies, salsa verde, black beans, salt, black pepper, and cilantro.

Lay tortillas on a clean, flat surface and spread on chicken mixture and Monterey Jack cheese. Fold in the sides and roll up the ends to secure.

Slice in halves and serve with guacamole, sour cream, and salsa.

Make it chimichanga:

Keep burritos whole.

Heat ½-inch of oil in a deep skillet and add two burritos. Fry for 3 minutes per side or until golden brown and crispy.

Transfer chimichangas to a paper towel-lined plate to drain grease. Fry the other two burritos the same way.

Serve with guacamole, sour cream, and salsa.

17. Pulled BBQ Pork Burritos / Chimichangas

If you've had BBQ pork anywhere else, you'll know that these wraps would be amazing. So, why not make them already?

Prep Time: 20 mins

Cook Time: 6 mins (chimichangas)

Serves: 4

Ingredients:

Burritos:

- 2 ½ cups pulled cooked pork shoulders
- ½ cup BBQ sauce, your favorite brand
- 4 large tortillas, burrito size
- 2 cups refried beans
- 1 cup shredded cheddar cheese
- 1 cup pico de gallo + extra for garnish
- ¼ cup chopped green chilies
- Sour cream, for serving
- Guacamole for serving

Chimichangas:

- Vegetable oil for frying
- Sour cream, for serving
- Guacamole for serving

Instructions:

Burritos:

In a bowl, mix pork with BBQ sauce until well-mixed.

Lay tortillas on a clean, flat surface and spread on refried beans. Add BBQ pork, cheddar cheese, pico de gallo, and green chilies. Fold in the sides and roll up the ends to secure.

Slice in halves, garnish with pico de gallo and serve with sour cream and guacamole.

Make it chimichanga:

Keep burritos whole.

Heat ½-inch of oil in a deep skillet and add two burritos. Fry for 3 minutes per side or until golden brown and crispy.

Transfer chimichangas to a paper towel-lined plate to drain grease. Fry the other two burritos the same way.

Garnish with pico de gallo and serve with sour cream and guacamole.

18. Taco Shrimp Burritos / Chimichangas

Boring shrimp burritos or chimichangas are a no-no. Pump things up with some taco seasoning and thank us later for the good outcome.

Prep Time: 20 mins

Cook Time: 4 mins (burritos) + 6 mins (chimichangas)

Serves: 4

Ingredients:

Burritos:

- 1 tbsp olive oil
- 1 lb. medium shrimp, peeled and deveined
- 1 tsp taco seasoning
- Salt to taste, if needed
- 4 large tortillas, burrito size
- 1 cup refried beans
- 1 cup shredded cheddar cheese
- Sour cream, pico de gallo, and chopped cilantro for serving

Chimichangas:

- Vegetable oil for frying
- Sour cream, pico de gallo, and chopped cilantro for serving

Instructions:

Burritos:

Heat olive oil in a skillet over medium heat. Season shrimp with taco seasoning and salt, if needed. Cook shrimp in oil for 1 to 2 minutes per side or until golden brown and opaque.

Lay tortillas on a clean, flat surface and spread refried beans. Top with shrimp and cheddar cheese. Fold in the sides and roll up the ends to secure.

Slice in halves and serve with sour cream, pico de gallo, and cilantro.

Make it chimichanga:

Keep burritos whole.

Heat ½-inch of oil in a deep skillet and add two burritos. Fry for 3 minutes per side or until golden brown and crispy.

Transfer chimichangas to a paper towel-lined plate to drain grease. Fry the other two burritos the same way.

Serve with sour cream, pico de gallo, and cilantro.

19. Green Chile Chicken Burritos / Chimichangas

Anyone up for spicy chicken? Green chilies have a lovely aroma, which overtakes these wraps. You'll love biting into them and guess what, they aren't painfully spicy.

Prep Time: 20 mins

Cook Time: 6 mins (chimichangas)

Serves: 4

Ingredients:

Burritos:

- 1 ½ cups shredded rotisserie chicken
- 1 large garlic clove, minced
- ½ navel orange, juiced
- ½ fresh lime juice
- 1 tsp cumin powder
- 1 (4 oz) can diced green chilies, drained
- 4 large tortillas, burrito size
- ½ cup shredded pepper jack cheese
- 1 (4 oz) can diced green chiles, drained
- 4 large tortillas, burrito size
- ½ cup shredded pepper jack cheese
- Pico de gallo for serving
- Sour cream for serving
- 1 avocado, pitted, peeled, and diced for serving
- Chopped fresh cilantro for serving

Chimichangas:

- Vegetable oil for frying
- Pico de gallo for serving
- Sour cream for serving
- 1 avocado, pitted, peeled, and diced for serving
- Chopped fresh cilantro for serving

Instructions:

Burritos:

In a bowl, combine chicken, garlic, orange juice, lime juice, cumin powder, and green chilies. Mix well.

Lay tortillas on a clean, flat surface and spread chicken on top and pepper jack cheese. Fold in the sides and roll up the ends to secure.

Slice in halves and serve with sour cream, pico de gallo, avocado, and cilantro.

Make it chimichanga:

Keep burritos whole.

Heat ½-inch of oil in a deep skillet and add two burritos. Fry for 3 minutes per side or until golden brown and crispy.

Transfer chimichangas to a paper towel-lined plate to drain grease. Fry the other two burritos the same way.

Serve with sour cream, pico de gallo, avocado, and cilantro.

20. Turkey Burritos / Chimichangas

Turkey is healthier than beef and tastier than chicken as they say. So, we are all in with some leftover turkey in these wraps.

Prep Time: 20 mins

Cook Time: 17 mins (burritos) + 6 mins (chimichangas)

Serves: 4

Ingredients:

Burritos:

- 2 tbsp olive oil
- ½ cup diced yellow onion
- 2 garlic cloves, minced
- 1 (15 oz) can diced tomatoes with green chilies
- 1 tablespoon chili powder
- 1 tbsp cumin powder
- ¼ tsp cayenne pepper (optional)
- 1 tbsp smoked paprika
- Salt and black pepper to taste
- 3 cups cooked shredded turkey
- ½ cup corn kernels, drained
- ½ cup chicken broth
- 4 large tortillas, burrito size
- 1 cup crumbled queso cheese + extra for garnish
- 2 tbsp chopped fresh cilantro
- Mixed salad greens for serving
- Pico de gallo for serving

Chimichangas:

- Vegetable oil for frying
- Mixed salad greens for serving
- Pico de gallo for serving

Instructions:

Burritos:

Heat olive oil in a skillet over medium heat. Add onion and sauté for 3 minutes. Stir in garlic and cook for 30 seconds or until fragrant. Stir in tomatoes, chili powder, cumin powder, paprika, cayenne pepper, salt, and black pepper. Cook for 10 minutes and stir in turkey, corn kernels, and broth. Simmer for 3 minutes to warm the turkey. Adjust taste with salt and black pepper.

Lay tortillas on a clean, flat surface and spread turkey mixture on top. Add queso cheese blend and cilantro. Fold in the sides and roll up the ends to secure.

Slice in halves, garnish with more queso cheese and serve with salad greens and pico de gallo.

Make it chimichanga:

Keep burritos whole.

Heat ½-inch of oil in a deep skillet and add two burritos. Fry for 3 minutes per side or until golden brown and crispy.

Transfer chimichangas to a paper towel-lined plate to drain grease. Fry the other two burritos the same way.

Garnish with more queso cheese and serve with salad greens and pico de gallo.

Serve warm.

21. Strawberry Cheesecake Burritos / Chimichangas

Let's get into the sweet treats by first making a strawberry cheesecake deconstruct that turns out amazing.

Prep Time: 20 mins

Cook Time: 6 mins (chimichangas)

Serves: 4

Ingredients:

Burritos:

- 1 (8 oz) package cream cheese, room temperature
- ¼ cup sour cream
- 1 tsp vanilla extract
- ¼ cup powdered sugar + extra for garnish
- ½ tsp fresh lemon zest
- 4 medium tortillas
- 1 ¾ cup sliced strawberries, divided
- Whipped cream for topping
- Fresh mint leaves for garnish

Chimichangas:

- Vegetable oil for frying
- Whipped cream for topping
- Fresh mint leaves for garnish

Instructions:

Burritos:

In a bowl, combine cream cheese, sour cream, vanilla, sugar, and lemon zest. Whisk until smooth and fold in ¾ cup of strawberries.

Lay tortillas on a clean, flat surface and spread cream cheese mixture on top. Fold in the sides and roll up the ends to secure.

Slice in halves and top with whipped cream. Garnish with remaining strawberries, some powdered sugar, and mint leaves. Serve.

Make it chimichanga:

Keep burritos whole.

Heat ½-inch of oil in a deep skillet and add two burritos. Fry for 3 minutes per side or until golden brown and crispy.

Transfer chimichangas to a paper towel-lined plate to drain grease. Fry the other two burritos the same way.

Garnish with remaining strawberries, some powdered sugar, and mint leaves. Serve.

22. Cherry Burritos / Chimichangas

No need to sweat dessert. Simply grab some cherry pie filling and make this effortless yet delicious treat.

Prep Time: 20 mins

Cook Time: 6 mins (chimichangas)

Serves: 4

Ingredients:

Burritos:

- 4 medium tortillas
- 1 cup cherry pie filling
- 1 tbsp cinnamon sugar

Chimichangas:

- Vegetable oil for frying

Instructions:

Burritos:

Lay tortillas on a clean, flat surface and spread cherry pie filling on top. Fold in the sides and roll up the ends to secure.

Slice in halves, garnish with cinnamon sugar and serve.

Make it chimichanga:

Keep burritos whole.

Heat ½-inch of oil in a deep skillet and add two burritos. Fry for 3 minutes per side or until golden brown and crispy.

Transfer chimichangas to a paper towel-lined plate to drain grease. Fry the other two burritos the same way.

Slice in halves, garnish with cinnamon sugar and serve.

23. Apple-Cinnamon Burritos/ Chimichangas

How pleasing? Again, we use some apple pie filling from the store, boosted it up with some cinnamon sugar and made it a happy thing for everyone.

Prep Time: 20 mins

Cook Time: 6 mins (chimichangas)

Serves: 4

Ingredients:

Burritos:

- 4 medium tortillas
- 1 cup apple pie filling
- 2 tbsp butter, melted
- ½ tbsp powdered sugar
- 1 tsp cinnamon powder

Chimichangas:

- Vegetable oil for frying

Instructions:

Burritos:

Lay tortillas on a clean, flat surface and spread cherry pie filling on top. Fold in the sides and roll up the ends to secure.

In a bowl, whisk butter, powdered sugar, and cinnamon powder until smooth.

Drizzle cinnamon butter on burritos and serve.

Make it chimichanga:

Keep burritos whole.

Heat ½-inch of oil in a deep skillet and add two burritos. Fry for 3 minutes per side or until golden brown and crispy.

Transfer chimichangas to a paper towel-lined plate to drain grease. Fry the other two burritos the same way.

Drizzle cinnamon butter on chimichangas and serve.

24. Quince and Manchego Burriots / Chimichangas

Quince and manchego cheese surprisingly pair well with each other. Grab a hearty bite and come back for more.

Prep Time: 20 mins

Cook Time: 6 mins (chimichangas)

Serves: 4

Ingredients:

Burritos:

- 4 medium tortillas
- 2 tbsp cinnamon sugar
- 1 cup quince paste
- 1 ½ cups shredded manchego cheese
- Caramel sauce for garnish

Chimichangas:

- Vegetable oil for frying
- Caramel sauce for garnish

Instructions:

Burritos:

Lay tortillas on a clean, flat surface and sprinkle cinnamon sugar on top. Spread on quince paste and manchego cheese. Fold in the sides and roll up the ends to secure.

Drizzle caramel sauce on top and serve.

Make it chimichanga:

Keep burritos whole.

Heat ½-inch of oil in a deep skillet and add two burritos. Fry for 3 minutes per side or until golden brown and crispy.

Transfer chimichangas to a paper towel-lined plate to drain grease. Fry the other two burritos the same way.

Drizzle caramel sauce on top and serve.

25. Creamed Pineapple Burritos / Chimichangas

Don't just have a bowl of pineapple today. Cream it up, stuff it into some tortillas and enjoy a more satisfying treat.

Prep Time: 20 mins

Cook Time: 6 mins (chimichangas)

Serves: 4

Ingredients:

Burritos:

- 1 (8 oz) package cream cheese, room temperature
- ¼ cup sour cream
- 1 tsp vanilla extract
- ¼ cup powdered sugar + extra for garnish
- ½ tsp fresh lemon zest
- 4 medium tortillas
- ¾ cup cubed pineapples
- Caramel sauce for garnish
- Toasted pecans for garnish

Chimichangas:

- Vegetable oil for frying
- Caramel sauce for garnish
- Toasted pecans for garnish

Instructions:

Burritos:

In a bowl, combine cream cheese, sour cream, vanilla, sugar, and lemon zest. Whisk until smooth and fold in ¾ cup of pineapples.

Lay tortillas on a clean, flat surface and spread creamed pineapple on top. Fold in the sides and roll up the ends to secure.

Slice in halves and drizzle caramel sauce on top. Garnish with pecans and serve.

Make it chimichanga:

Keep burritos whole.

Heat ½-inch of oil in a deep skillet and add two burritos. Fry for 3 minutes per side or until golden brown and crispy.

Transfer chimichangas to a paper towel-lined plate to drain grease. Fry the other two burritos the same way.

Slice in halves and drizzle caramel sauce on top. Garnish with pecans and serve.

26. Ice Cream Burritos / Chimichangas

While enjoying ice cream is a treat in itself, it doesn't hurt to be extra about it. So, here we managed to stuff some tortillas with ice cream, sprinkled on some cinnamon sugar and it worked.

Prep Time: 20 mins

Cook Time: 6 mins (chimichangas) + 2 hours freezing

Serves: 4

Ingredients:

Burritos:

- 4 medium tortillas
- 2 cups vanilla ice cream
- ½ cup cinnamon sugar

Chimichangas:

- Vegetable oil for frying

Instructions:

Burritos:

Lay tortillas on a clean, flat surface and top with ice cream. Fold in the sides and roll up the ends to secure.

Place in a dish and freeze for 2 hours.

After, sprinkle with cinnamon sugar and serve.

Make it chimichanga:

Keep burritos whole after freezing.

Heat ½-inch of oil in a deep skillet and add two burritos. Fry for 3 minutes per side or until golden brown and crispy.

Transfer chimichangas to a paper towel-lined plate to drain grease. Fry the other two burritos the same way.

Sprinkle with cinnamon sugar and serve.

27. Nutella Banana Burritos / Chimichangas

So, we made a breakfast/dessert treat with this set because nearly everyone loves Nutella. We added some fruits and called it a day.

Prep Time: 20 mins

Cook Time: 6 mins (chimichangas)

Serves: 4

Ingredients:

Burritos:

- 4 medium tortillas
- 3 tbsp Nutella + extra for garnish
- 2 fresh bananas, peeled and sliced + extra for garnish
- 1 strawberry, sliced for garnish (optional)
- Powdered sugar for garnish

Chimichangas:

- Vegetable oil for frying
- Sliced banana for garnish
- Sliced strawberry for garnish (optional)
- Powdered sugar for garnish

Instructions:

Burritos:

Lay tortillas on a clean, flat surface and spread Nutella on top. Add bananas and fold in the sides and roll up the ends to secure.

Drizzle more Nutella on top and garnish with some banana slices, strawberry, and powdered sugar.

Serve.

Make it chimichanga:

Keep burritos whole.

Heat ½-inch of oil in a deep skillet and add two burritos. Fry for 3 minutes per side or until golden brown and crispy.

Transfer chimichangas to a paper towel-lined plate to drain grease. Fry the other two burritos the same way.

Drizzle more Nutella on top and garnish with some banana slices, strawberry, and powdered sugar.

Serve.

28. Milk Chocolate Burritos / Chimichangas

What is your favorite milk chocolate? Okay, stuff some tortillas with it and enjoy. That simple but amazing.

Prep Time: 20 mins

Cook Time: 6 mins (chimichangas)

Serves: 4

Ingredients:

Burritos:

- 4 medium tortillas
- ¼ cup cinnamon sugar
- 1 cup milk chocolate chips, melted
- Powdered sugar for garnish

Chimichangas:

- Vegetable oil for frying
- 4 medium tortillas
- ¼ cup cinnamon sugar
- Powdered sugar for garnish

Instructions:

Burritos:

Lay tortillas on a clean, flat surface and sprinkle cinnamon sugar on top. Drizzle on milk chocolate. Fold in the sides and roll up the ends to secure.

Slice in halves, dust with powdered sugar and serve.

Make it chimichanga:

Heat ½-inch of oil in a deep skillet.

Lay tortillas on a clean, flat surface. Sprinkle cinnamon sugar on top and add milk chocolate chips. Fold in the sides and roll up the ends to secure.

Place two burritos in hot oil and fry for 3 minutes per side or until golden brown and crispy.

Transfer chimichangas to a paper towel-lined plate to drain grease. Fry the other two burritos the same way.

Slice in halves, dust with powdered sugar and serve.

29. Creamed Berries Burritos. Chimichangas

Berries are naturally a dessert-thing but when you add some cream and white chocolate, you know you've hit a really good mark. You get that here.

Prep Time: 20 mins

Cook Time: 6 mins (chimichangas)

Serves: 4

Ingredients:

Burritos:

- 1 (8 oz) package cream cheese, room temperature
- ¼ cup sour cream
- 1 tsp vanilla extract
- ¼ cup powdered sugar + extra for garnish
- ½ tsp fresh lemon zest
- 4 medium tortillas
- ¾ cup mixed berries, strawberries chopped or sliced
- White chocolate syrup for topping

Chimichangas:

- Vegetable oil for frying
- White chocolate syrup for topping

Instructions:

Burritos:

In a bowl, combine cream cheese, sour cream, vanilla, sugar, and lemon zest. Whisk until smooth and fold in berries.

Lay tortillas on a clean, flat surface and spread cream cheese mixture on top. Fold in the sides and roll up the ends to secure.

Slice in halves, swirl white chocolate syrup and serve.

Make it chimichanga:

Keep burritos whole.

Heat ½-inch of oil in a deep skillet and add two burritos. Fry for 3 minutes per side or until golden brown and crispy.

Transfer chimichangas to a paper towel-lined plate to drain grease. Fry the other two burritos the same way.

Slice in halves, swirl white chocolate syrup and serve.

30. Apricot Jam Burritos / Chimichangas

What creamy goodness we have here with a very impressive touch of apricots. Bite in and repeat.

Prep Time: 20 mins

Cook Time: 6 mins (chimichangas)

Serves: 4

Ingredients:

Burritos:

- 4 medium tortillas
- 4 oz cream cheese, room temperature
- 1 cup apricot jam
- Whipped cream for garnish

Chimichangas:

- Vegetable oil for frying

Instructions:

Burritos:

Lay tortillas on a clean, flat surface and spread cream cheese on top, then apricot jam. Fold in the sides and roll up the ends to secure.

Slice in halves, garnish with whipped cream and serve.

Make it chimichanga:

Keep burritos whole.

Heat ½-inch of oil in a deep skillet and add two burritos. Fry for 3 minutes per side or until golden brown and crispy.

Transfer chimichangas to a paper towel-lined plate to drain grease. Fry the other two burritos the same way.

Slice in halves, garnish with whipped cream and serve.

Conclusion

What's more? Nothing really than to get into making them and enjoying whole-heartedly.

These burritos and chimichangas would make anyone smile so we hope you get to share them even as you enjoy them.

Cheers!

Biography

"Cooking is a chore unless you love the process", which is the motto of Tyler Sweet, an extremely talented chef who has made her name in the catering industry with the help of her deep understanding of a variety of ingredients and human taste buds. She had always loved whipping up new recipes as a pass time activity but her career began when she got her first job at a local restaurant and realized that she would not mind doing it forever.

Tyler's hobby blossomed into a passion that drove her up the ladder so quickly that by the end of the year, she was already a sous chef and a rising talent. An impeccable eye for unique mixtures and a willingness to learn new dishes, she has since then worked for over 10 five-star restaurants in the tri-state. Presently, Sweet owns a thriving online cooking class where she has found a great, interactive avenue to teach on her most favorite subject, food.

Author's Note

I really appreciate you taking the time to not just download but also read my book, you don't know but that is the highest compliment you can ever give me. And it may seem greedy but I just have one more favor to ask of you, I need your feedback. Do you have any comments, suggestions, or complaints? Or you have an idea for my next book? Please reach out to me if you like, I'm always available for my loyal readers.

Thank you.

Tyler Sweet

Made in the USA
Columbia, SC
04 January 2023